STEPRO

NOTHING BUT LIFE

NOTHING BUT LIFE

"Photography is truth."

— Jean-Luc Godard

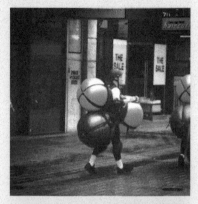

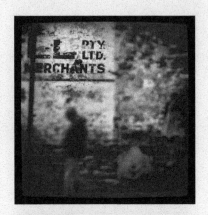

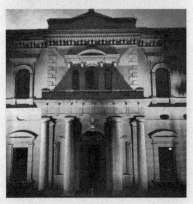

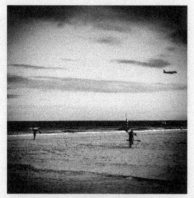

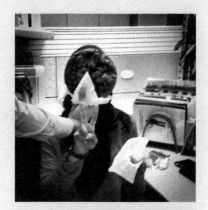

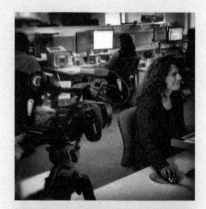

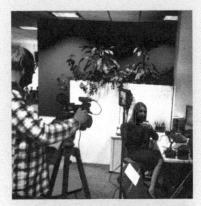

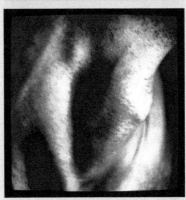

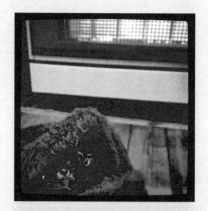

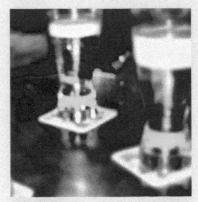

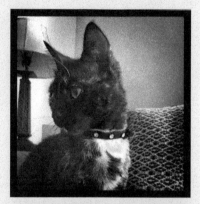

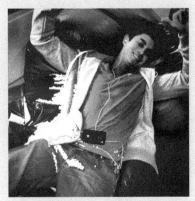

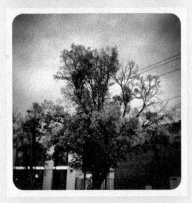

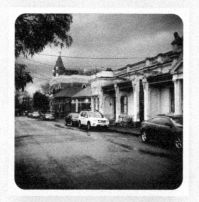

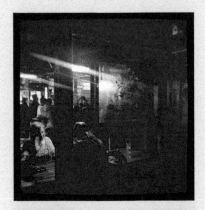

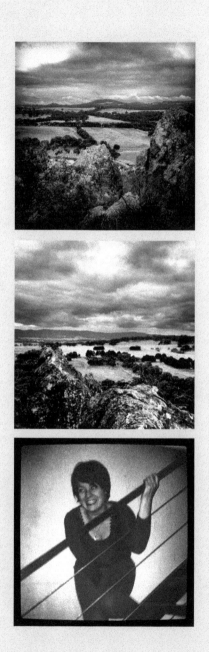

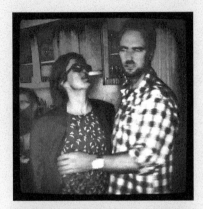

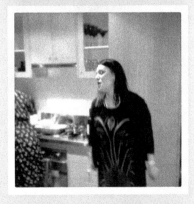

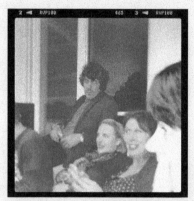

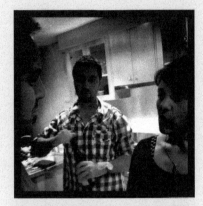

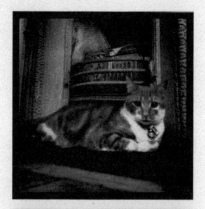

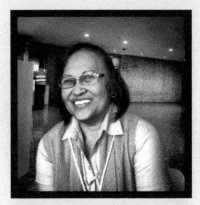

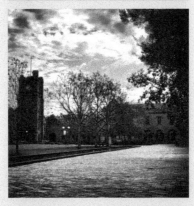

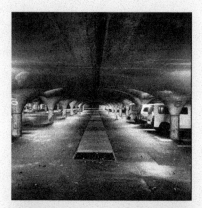

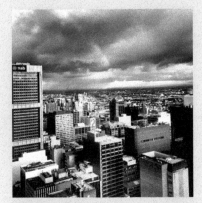

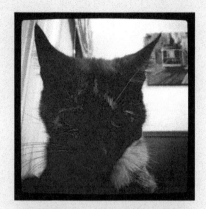

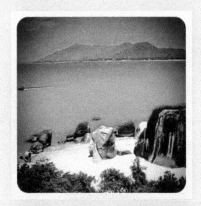

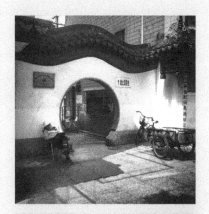

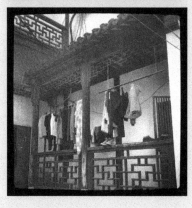

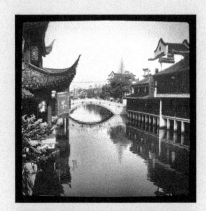

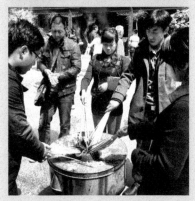

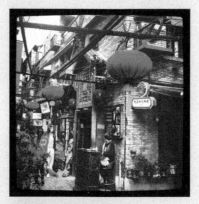

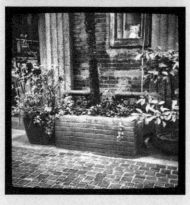

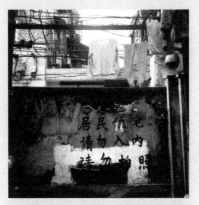

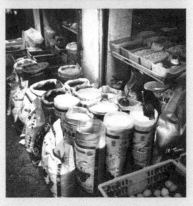

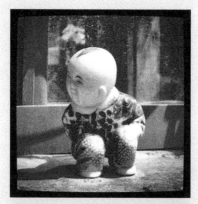

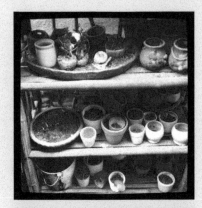

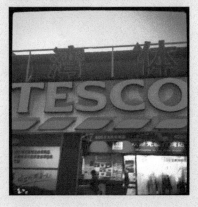

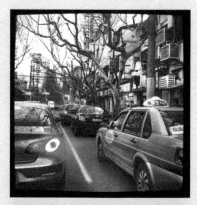

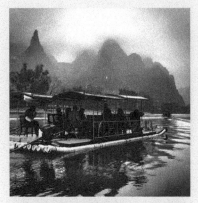

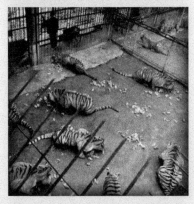

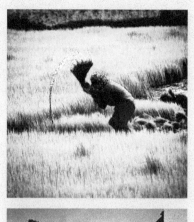

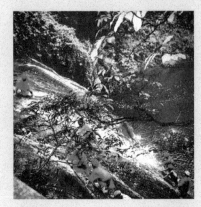

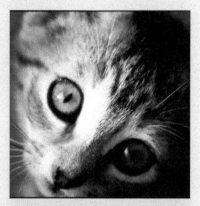

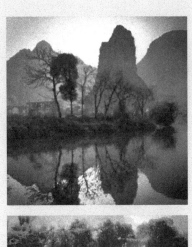

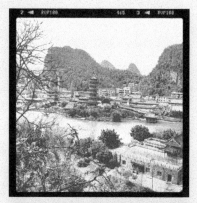

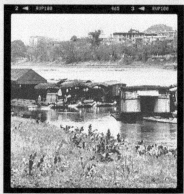

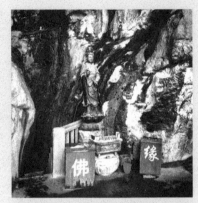

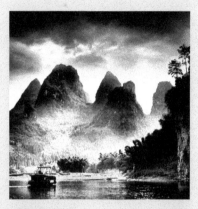

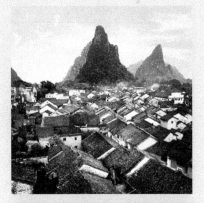

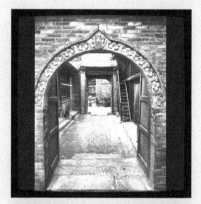

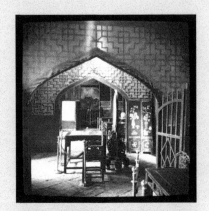

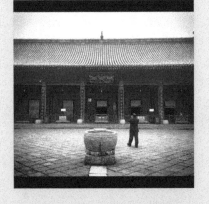

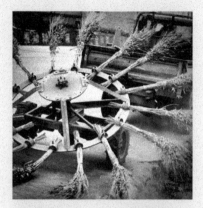

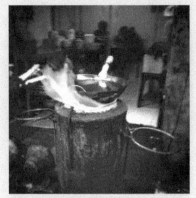

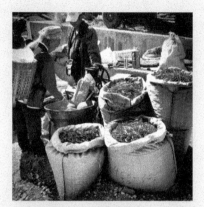

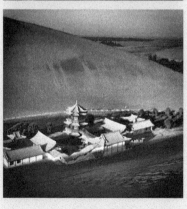

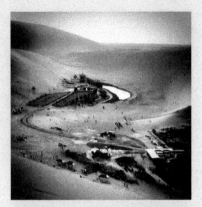

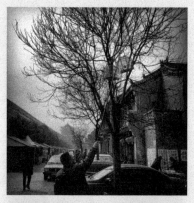

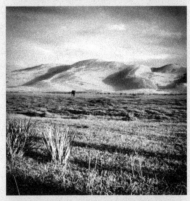

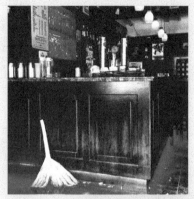

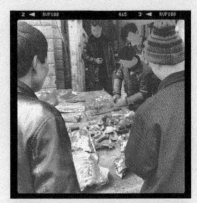

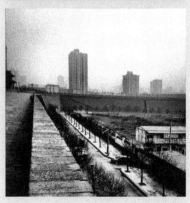

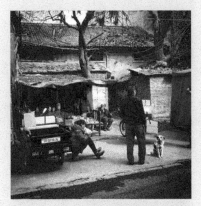

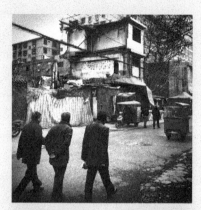

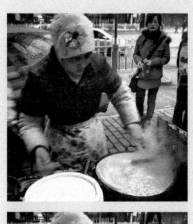

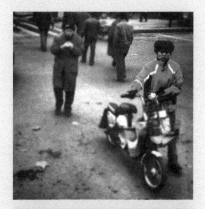

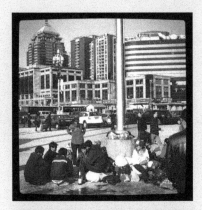

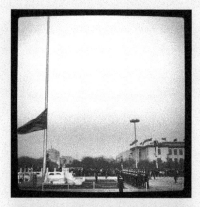

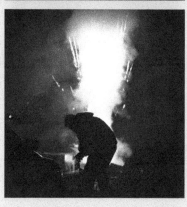

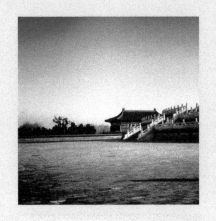

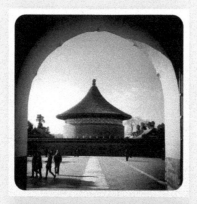

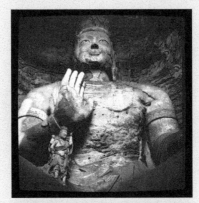

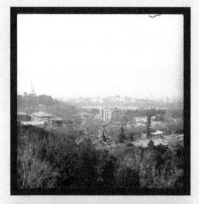

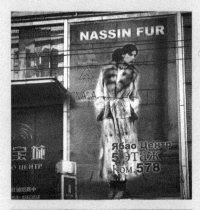

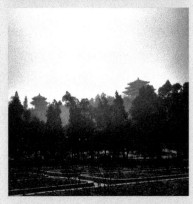

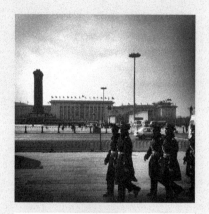

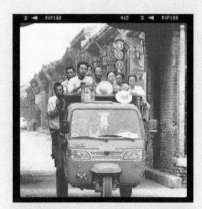

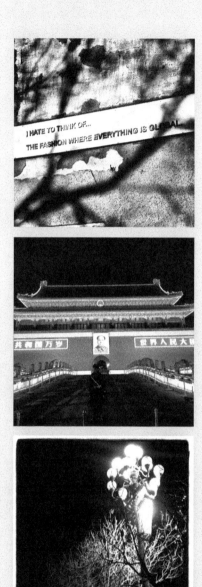

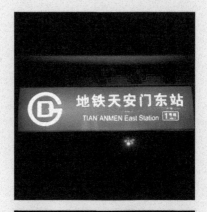

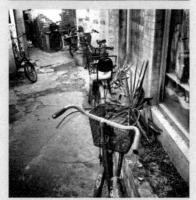

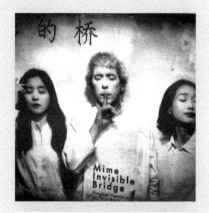

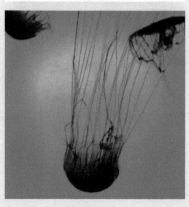

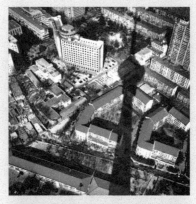

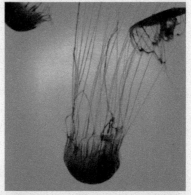

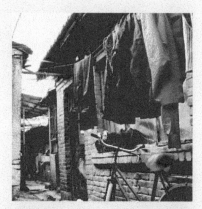

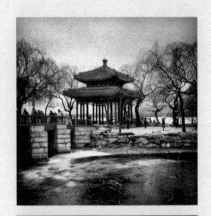

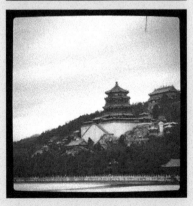

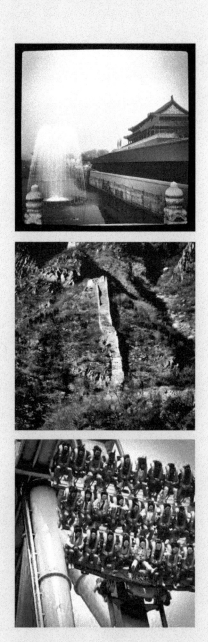

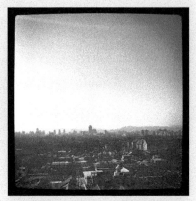

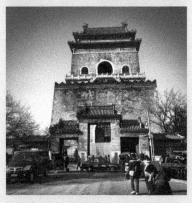

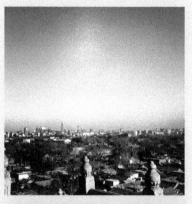

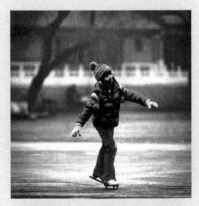

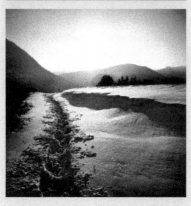

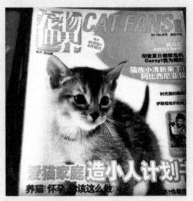

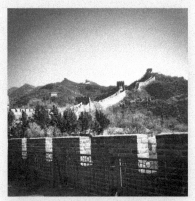

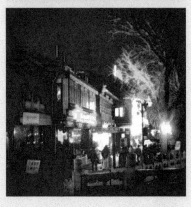

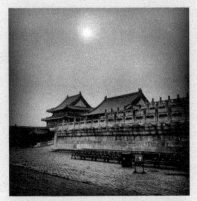

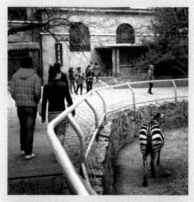

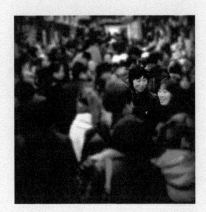

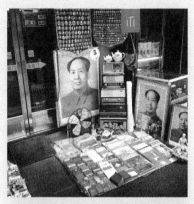

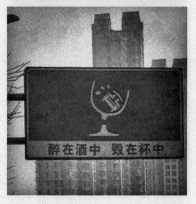

醉在酒中　毀在杯中

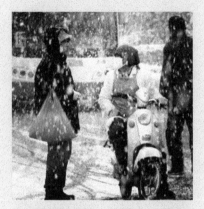

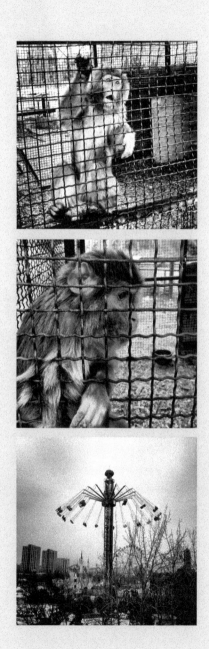

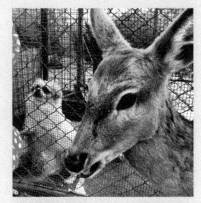

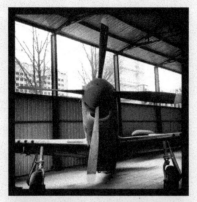

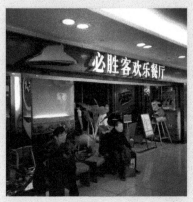

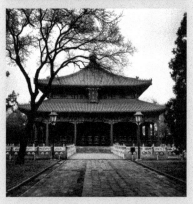

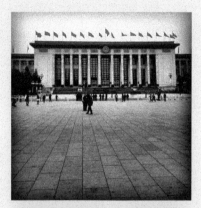

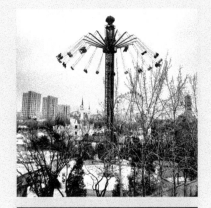

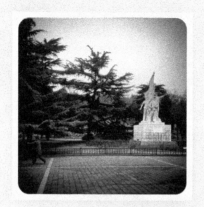

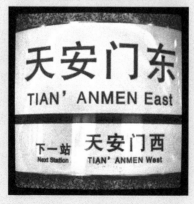

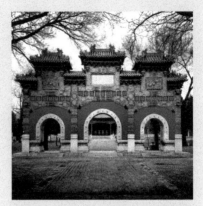

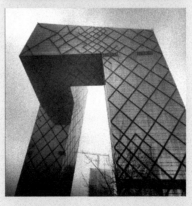

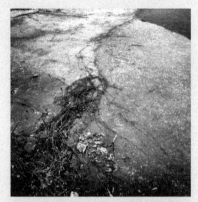

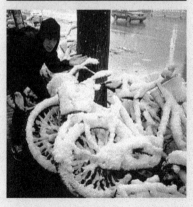

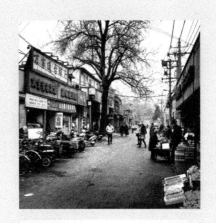

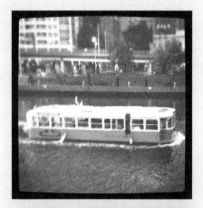

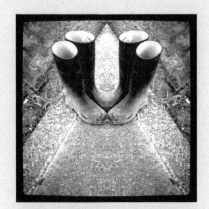

2 ◄ RVP100   465   3 ◄ RVP100

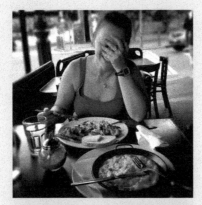

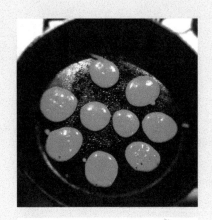

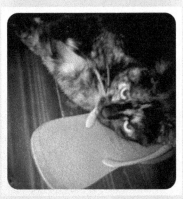

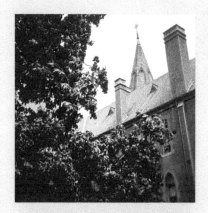

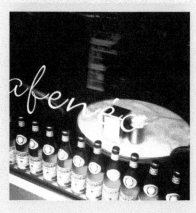

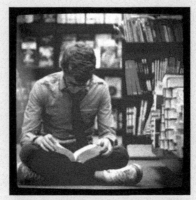

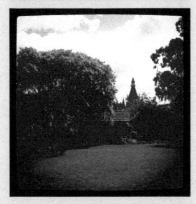

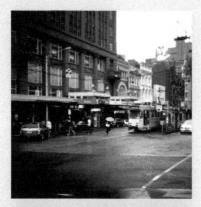

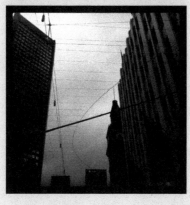

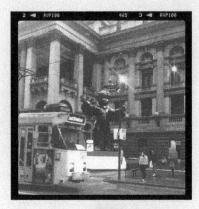

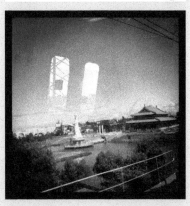

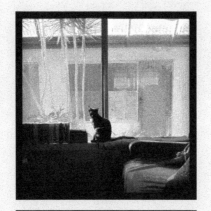

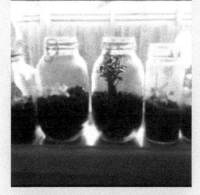

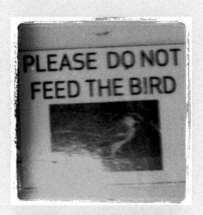

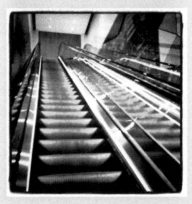

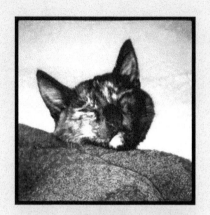

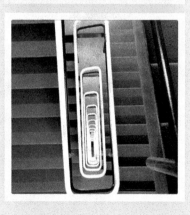

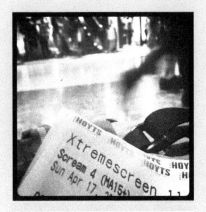

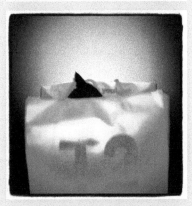

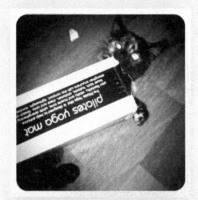

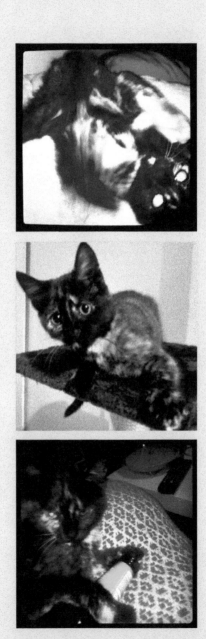

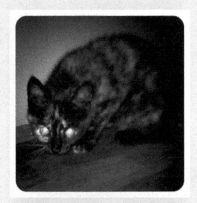

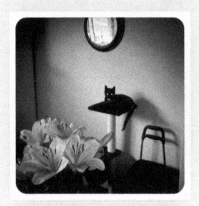

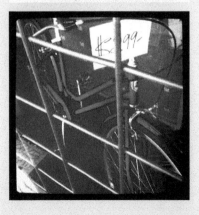

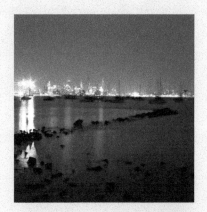

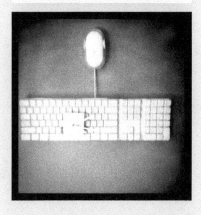

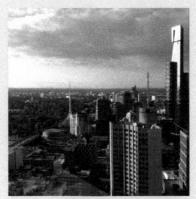

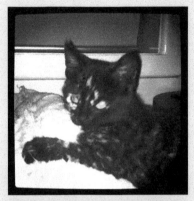

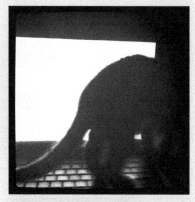

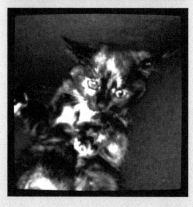

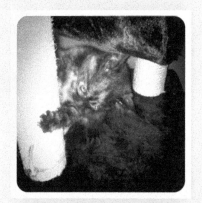

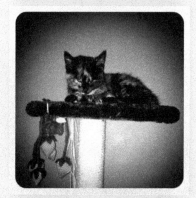

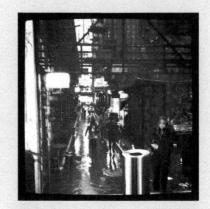

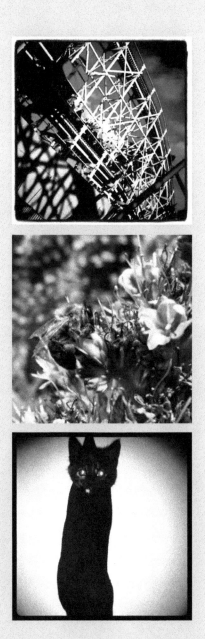

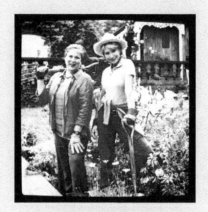

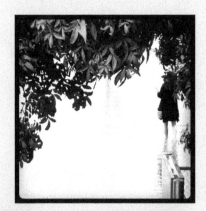

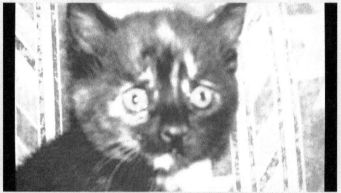

CPSIA information can be obtained
at www.ICGtesting.com
Printed in the USA
BVHW050530210819
556237BV00025B/181/P

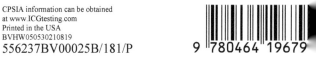